BOA
EDITIONS LTD

Beautiful in the Mouth
by
Keetje Kuipers

Winner, 2009 A. Poulin, Jr. Poetry Prize
Selected by Thomas Lux

Beautiful in the Mouth

Poems by
Keetje Kuipers

Foreword by Thomas Lux

A. POULIN, JR. NEW POETS OF AMERICA SERIES, NO. 32

BOA Editions, Ltd.   ❧   Rochester, NY   ❧   2010

First Edition
10 11 12 13   7 6 5 4 3 2 1

For information about permission to reuse any material from this book please contact The
Permissions Company at www.permissionscompany.com or e-mail permdude@eclipse.net.

Publications by BOA Editions, Ltd.—a not-for-profit corporation under section 501 (c) (3)
of the United States Internal Revenue Code—are made possible with funds from a variety of
sources, including public funds from the New York State Council on the Arts, a state agency;
the Literature Program of the National Endowment for the Arts; the County of Monroe,
NY; the Lannan Foundation for support of the Lannan Translations Selection Series; the
Sonia Raiziss Giop Charitable Foundation; the Mary S. Mulligan Charitable Trust; the
Rochester Area Community Foundation; the Arts & Cultural Council for Greater Roches-
ter; the Steeple-Jack Fund; the Ames-Amzalak Memorial Trust in memory of Henry Ames,
Semon Amzalak and Dan Amzalak; and contributions from many individuals nationwide.
See Colophon on page 96 for special individual acknowledgments.

Cover Design: Sandy Knight
Cover Art: "Phoenix for Gordon" by Frank Boyden
Interior Design and Composition: Richard Foerster
Manufacturing: BookMobile
BOA Logo: Mirko

Library of Congress Cataloging-in-Publication Data

Kuipers, Keetje.
  Beautiful in the mouth / by Keetje Kuipers. — 1st ed.
      p. cm. — (A. Poulin, Jr. new poets of America series ; no. 32)
  ISBN 978-1-934414-33-0 (pbk. : alk. paper)
  I. Title.
  PS3611.U4B43 2010
  811'.6—dc22
                                    2009028300

BOA Editions, Ltd.
Thom Ward, Editor/Production
Peter Conners, Editor/Marketing
Melissa Hall, Development Director/Office Manager
Bernadette Catalana, BOA Board Chair
A. Poulin, Jr., Founder (1938–1996)
250 North Goodman Street, Suite 306
Rochester, NY 14607
www.boaeditions.org

NATIONAL
ENDOWMENT
FOR THE ARTS
A great nation
deserves great art.

State of the Arts

NYSCA

Contents

III

IV

V

Foreword

Keetje Kuipers, or the speaker of her poems ("And speaker, // coded "'you'"), has lived in several places: Minnesota, Montana, Washington, Oregon, California, Pennsylvania. She has also lived in New York City and has written some of the most powerful and emotional, as well as literal, descriptions of life in that particularly American place that I have read since, well, Hart Crane and Lorca. Where she's from, exactly, I don't know. A suburb somewhere, she or her speaker says. Where she lives now: don't know. Is Keetje Kuipers her real name? Probably, but it doesn't matter. Her poems do matter, resoundingly in many cases, always in one way or another.

On my first reading of the manuscript I was immediately struck by her imaginative powers. I was delighted by how original her poems were and yet how accessible, how they were always connected to something recognizably human and alive, despite their numerous turns, leaps, dazzling metaphors and similes, and passionate syntax.

It seems she understands down to her bone marrow what our great mother of American poetry, Emily Dickinson, said when she wrote, "Tell all the truth but tell it slant." Sometimes her poems remind me of the anguish and strength of Marina Tsvetaeva. Like all poets, she probably has many influences, and, like all good poets, she has absorbed their lessons, assimilated them into a voice entirely her own.

Kuipers has also learned her trade: her poems are tight but loaded. There are a handful of traditional sonnets, each beautifully tuned, made so well that you might not know they are sonnets on first reading, which is the point of the craft, of a received form: to do its job, not to announce itself. She has a splendid ear—there are all sorts of sound-bounces, internal rhyme, assonance, as well as end rhyme, in these poems. She uses all the tools a poet has: I've mentioned her use of metaphor and simile (seemingly undervalued these days, and they made Plato nervous a long time ago, but to me quintessential poetic tools) and add to these onomatopoeia, oxymoron, synaesthesia. Kuipers never grabs the reader by the lapels with these tools and shouts, "Here I am, Mr. Oxymoron!" Nope. She uses the tools of her trade to do what they're supposed to do, which is to help the poem get under the reader's skin, into the reader's heart.

Keetje Kuipers' poems are the real deal, folks. Read them at your peril. Read them for your joy.

—Thomas Lux

For Max, on whatever bright subway train he rides

I

The Light Behind Her Head, the Bright Honeycomb of the Sky

At night his long body works above me,
late into the hours that make themselves
from dust, crafting the landscape out of midnight's cloth,
pulling Stockholm from behind the moon,
its blue skies rendered in Delft ink,
the cobblestone piers that part the water
at its glistening seams, and then the summer

evenings on the Hudson, a New York
he's making in my legs now, those runs past Ellis
Island, our lady of liberty swung out
beside Tribeca's ragged shoulder,
her fragile skyline shaped with dusk's gold filigree.
There are the deaths that terrify me still

because they have not happened yet. He'll wash
them from my eyes with Japan and all her
colored scarves wrapped around the limbs of trees
that forget themselves in blossoming.
Like the flowering corset that is the world
doing up her stays each morning, shaping
herself again to hold us all in semiprecious light.

Between Dreams of My Country

My mother sleeps in the bed beside me.
Out the window, graduated light
seems to snowcap each tall building.
And though I've tried to explain it to her,
this my American city, in a way
that might appear true, even to myself—
the god-black nights suspended above us
in the taut and trembling shape
of a forgotten tent top, the rats behind
my walls pushing the gray flesh of their feet
into our gristle and rails, the inhabitants
who cannot see the bright graffiti
and the travelers who stare—
how truly unsure I am when I speak.

And what I've left behind: the star-smoked
skies, a pint of red beer floating
in my hand, and me wanting to shatter
something without the sound of breaking glass.
Throwing myself from the prairie's golden boat
became a way of saying, *Enough safe harbor.*
The city stops at the water's edge and no
bridge can extend its life. Its streets
alluvial, its very bones soaked in the mud
that makes stone into gem: bright pith,
tender core. When do I get to call you home?
She sleeps and sleeps, and I let her go on
like that. It's not right yet. It's not yet day.

Remembering Our Last Meal in New York

I eat *chirashizushi*, peel the raw fish
from their sweet bed of seasoned rice.
I know right now the beaten mares on 59th
stomp slowly at the snowy curb, take great
pitchers of air into their distended lungs
and bloom from between yellowed teeth
white peonies against the trees of Central Park.
I have tried to forget your light, the way it breaks
me open, even now, and makes me speak,
how it glitters in the gutters up and down Eighth Avenue,
swirling in pools of snowmelt, so many
sparkling tea leaves I still read for signs of you.

Driving Back into the City

Here's what I'm trying to say: the deer coming toward us through the dark,
  and us not seeing them,

the car flying over the bridge into the maw of the city like a willing moth
  suddenly wrapped in fire,

the cabs rushing downtown like yellow-winged beetles, bearing the beat
  of many shuddering hearts.

Everything just as we left it: the skyline arching its neck on the horizon,
  still growing its spine of suckled spikes,

the key slowly clicking in the lock until the door swings open to dinner plates
  stacked like scoured turtle shells,

the footprints around the bed unfolding constellations, opening patiently
  against the floor.

And our thighs rocking together like two moored boats in the night,
  all those tender lights held tight in their hulls.

There is only one way to say this: We move in the night toward something
  other than ourselves,

never knowing the eyes that bloom around us, only these words holding up
  the thin air we breathe.

Self-Portrait with Cockroach

Trespass is what we say
when we mean willful: a covert

footprint you leave outside
her bedroom window: when

harm's been done: an unlawful
tampering, a body marked:

what keeps you up all night
listening to the neighbor

call in his cats: oh, the animals
we might choose to save, put them

on a polystyrene ark to Mars: what
we start that finishes us: the seventy-

four degree day in December:
ice-cream trucks parked outside

our tall buildings: air conditioners
buzzing: your hands sticky

with cream and sugar: the last
frozen objects on earth: our little

experiment, our vanity project
gone awry: side effects: the forced

music of your body's slapping
rhythm when it lands against

your lover: how you do love her:
your sun, your moon: your

carbon: that prison of molecules
you call flesh: an insect, a bug:

dirty light: no light at all:
a wave as well as a particle.

Bondage Play as a Substitute for Prayer

Slack bodies need a chain, a tightening.

Because I have a good life,
because the scales are tipped too far
toward my own contentment, I ask my man
to put his hands around my wicker throat
and squeeze. I'm familiar with the consequences
of happiness: When we become too easy in our lives,
god doesn't waste his time making an example of us.
Better that I take my beating from a hand
I love. When beauty and pleasure cling
to my staticed legs, when fortune's grotesque
and comely filaments cloud my hair,
I know to ask for pain.
                            Without the wick of wire,
I fear god-on-earth, his deep hands churning
through the most tender porches of my body,
the shadows he commands my fine rails
cast. I'll take my punishment from my man
or this bed becomes my unlacquered black ocean,
my bottomless potato field, my factory floor
where unseen hands hold me down,
my church where I can't even say, *Yes, hit me.*

There's only so much goodness one body can hold.

Finding Out I'm Pregnant

Last night New York put on its lights,
shouldered up the dusk like a mantle
of thick cashmere or a garland of plumeria
heavy with scent. Now here we are
at an ocean's mouth, watching animals leave
the hard ground for water, the dark
river named for a distant country
we can't see. You slip into me again. A seal
enters the water with all its gentle weight.
The waves darn a lace ribbon along the edge
of the dock, stones rising like Russian monoliths
stained white with cormorant droppings.
We are gone as the lights come on far away:
the egg that bursts through, the magnolia
fired with purple glaze, the hands that cup
themselves inside me. Like infinite mouths
opening to show their teeth, the cadenced surf
shines uncontrollably. Watch me drop
from the dock, become the slip—soundless—
of a body swimming inside a body.

Diagnosis

There are a variety of ways to respond
to despair: drinking, weeping, picking
fights in bars. I took a lover under
the stairwell of a brownstone
at a party in Brooklyn. It was winter,
had been a week of buttoned collars
and long, black coats, of the nurses
from St. Vincent's taking their cigarette
breaks huddled against the hoods
of ambulances, pale blue scrubs flapping
at their knees, of hotdog vendors working
stiff bottles of ketchup and mustard
in their gloved hands, of corner
bodega roses frozen fast in their
buckets of water. It was also the week
I learned my body could do itself harm,
arriving at the doctor's office, cheeks
bitten red by cold, the nurse saying, *Sit down.*
All I remember from that party
were his hands moving in quick dressage
under my blouse, the tangled carousels
of dust motes falling from the stairs
above our heads, and how every time
I wanted to cry out instead I made that
tender bird of desire nestle in my mouth.
All bodies hold secrets. My lover's armpits
were whittled ampersand hollows. I clutched
at the spaces that were not there.

Santeria for the City: Blackout, Summer 2003

This is what you must do first:
Peel the dragon fruit skin
from its flesh, separate pink
from pink. This last day
is ritual you've learned, how to say
goodbye more completely,
how to banish what is loved.

The refrigerator must be emptied
and every pancetta risotto persimmon
that you bought in Little Italy China Town
Union Square, once wrapped
in sodden paper and pressed
into your hand, must be devoured,
finished, the core or rind
laid on the sill for pigeons and rats,
the headless that arrive and depart the city's limits
each day, shadows on the wall
of a tunnel filled with hurtling
and plundered light.

As the body is a home,
as the city is a body,
as circuitry runs the lengths
of my arms, these streets—we are a flash
in the fuse box, a blown kiss
into blackness, the perfect thrill
of your last departure
orbiting its small plane inside you.

II

Why I Live West of the Rockies

When I said I didn't want to live in
Pennsylvania, I meant it. The house out-
side Philadelphia rotting each limb
that's lost its use, your mother's soldered pout
as she hands over the china, wrinkled
hills of leafless trees spreading a browned gown,
the sparse lights of the Ivy Leagues sprinkled
on the horizon, academe gone down
like a fast ship on fire—You could never
understand why I won't go back. Like all
shadows, our history's carved by weather-
bent sun. Against us, all the seasons. Fall,
then winter shortening our lives with bone
white snow, the home it will find over stone.

On Earth As It Is in Heaven

Our great storytellers are all dead,
      but what they've left us—

      a god for every star in heaven—

remains enough. We pray and are comforted
      by the sound of our own voices,

      satisfied with echoes. The wasps, too,

have a god, their queen whose children
      pass among us, and bring her gifts

      of the living—fat squirming cousins

they clutch to their bellies, so heavy
      they can hardly fly: beetle, termite,

      spider, bee. They constellate

the summer's blue sky with their freighted
      flight, each quivering, meaty

      sacrifice struggling to break free

and plummet back to the earth of dead
      grass and dandelion dander. If one

      should escape—oh, rare and worthless

reprieve, like nickels dropped in a deepening
        coffer—its myth would tell of clasping,

      wings, a fierce and all-consuming

hum as it was lifted higher into the light,
        and a fear as well, which it now mistakes

      in the brief leisure of retrospect, for ecstasy.

What We Call Indian Summer

Last night, moths commanded by candle flame
hovered at my elbows like fat but agile bartenders.
Now the grasshoppers continue their whittling gait
through the tall grass and each hour of the shortening day
the low sun plays a different tune on the accordion of light
made by slim trees at the meadow's edge. Yes, it's true,
I haven't thought about what it might mean for everything
to stay the same, just a continuation of disappearances,
like chainsaws early in the morning, distant and harmless.
Wouldn't I be frightened if they returned each summer—
the magnificent corn castles of my Minnesota girlhood—
and I could step into them again, still holding my father's hand,
him stooping through the doorway that remains
just at my height? There's nothing to stop us but the snow.
And if it doesn't fall, what then of my plan for forgiveness?
Being in the future, it wavers on a radio frequency
I can't pick up here in the endless present where I have night
after night of full moons and crumbled butter moths.

To the Bear Who Ate a Ten-Pound Bag of Sunflower Seeds in My Front Yard This Morning

When I lived in New York, and of course you
can't know this, or even understand
what I mean by *New York*—its lonesome
singular glow on the horizon as I came
by bus across the New Jersey marsh,
the lights just as humbling as those I saw last week
when driving the back roads after midnight
I passed an incandescent cow milking parlor,
beasts rustling in their stalls, an island
like a hollowed-out flame—everything was hard
to come by. The bodies on the street
contracted against the cold or the smell of stained
pavement, and most of all, always each other.
The January I moved to the city, there were four
blizzards. My lover rode the train in on weekends
and we left the apartment only for sweaty, thin slices
they sold on the corner or the occasional bottle of wine.
We were always hungry, and it seemed ineffable to us,
what it was we wanted, and then, of course,
whether or not we could have it. I see that in you now,
the way you hoard your pile of stolen seeds,
your resistance, that glum desire. When we took things—
like the man I once saw run out the door
of the Associated Grocery on 103rd, canned goods
dropping from his pockets and into the snow banks,
the heavy tuna and soup making neat little shafts
where the light shone only dimly on their
aluminum tops—they felt earned.

River Sonnet

When the old she-salmon swam to my rock
where I had sat to watch her moldering
transform into a fruiting body, clock
of flesh stretched above pale pebbles, ticking
tail where her roe lay like scattered apple
blossoms the rain adhered to the road,
and her great heaving sides stained with the dull
flowering shapes of fungus, I could not know
what secret pain it took for her to nose
against the current there, the large head scarred,
flanks those of a barnacled ship: she rose
from shallow water, a calcified shard
bearing time's white etchings, and one dark eye—
lidless—that willed I mark her drifting by.

Blackfoot River

Wading the river in near-darkness, the valley
still close from the smoky fires burning
twenty miles east, my brother turns to me
and says, *I'm telling you this for your own good.*
Later, I won't remember what it is he says
but only that we've crawled under a taut line
of barbed wire, that the black cows in the farmer's field
are just suggestions of themselves, that the smoke
gnaws the color from the sky.

I have a lover four hundred miles away and when
we try to speak there's only darkness, like two
dogs pointing into a stand of trees at where they've heard
the promise of sound, though what they hear is only
an outline—not actually what stands among the boughs.
Now the thin trestle of my brother's shoulders is all
I can see moving in front of me as we near the truck
and I wonder what I'll do when he disappears.

Soon we're drinking Millers as we drive past
the smokejumper camps, out on gravel roads where
we honk the horn to scatter deer, try to save something
that doesn't know us. When we pull up to the house—
buzzed and tired, smelling of fish—I can see my parents in there
lighting cigarettes in the dark. I think this means we must
want to die, despite everything we say. And what are we moving
towards in speech except more words that waste their motion?
The unspeakable spoken and spoken until it becomes
lost in the bright keening of the stars, those unknown
latitudes we measure every message against.

All the things I'm afraid to say, about the dog
no one's cleared from the side of the road, how I see
the young boys crossing under the wire fence each dusk—
where do they go? Words do not do the work. We're all
liars. Better to keep silent, wait to see the beast
we've heard in among the trees. But oh my god the owl,
crossing the dim orb of that stained moon. It must be criminal
the way I stand around and watch.

The Reno

You never take me to the bar next to the trailer park
        so I don't know if the men stand in circles

at the pockmarked counter, or if the women have their hair
        done in curls. I like to imagine that I could be

one of them, that you could be the man brushing fine
        shuffleboard sand from his fingertips, a hidden

birthmark like buckshot on your belly. The mirror
        in the bathroom might be cracked or scrawled

with a Merle Haggard lyric: *Ain't no woman gonna change*
        the way I think. But from here all I can see is neon

going on and off in the rain, the puddles in the parking lot
        splashing back the blinking marquee: *Food. Beer. Jukebox.*

A place to lift a cold glass to my lips and disappear
        the last of the gold down my throat. Just beyond

our trailer, the sound of trains hitching and unhitching
        is thunder entering my ribs and I want it.

Across a Great Wilderness Without You

The deer come out in the evening.
God bless them for not judging me,
I'm drunk. I stand on the porch in my bathrobe
and make strange noises at them—
                              language,
if language can be a kind of crying.
The tin cans scattered in the meadow glow,
each bullet hole suffused with moon,
like the platinum thread beyond them
where the river runs the length of the valley.
That's where the fish are.
                              Tomorrow
I'll scoop them from the pockets of graveled
stone beneath the bank, their bodies
desperately alive when I hold them in my hands,
the way prayers become more hopeless
when uttered aloud.
                    The phone's disconnected.
Just as well, I've got nothing to tell you:
I won't go inside where the bats dip and swarm
over my bed. It's the sound of them
shouldering against each other that terrifies me,
as if it might hurt to brush across another being's
living flesh.
              But I carry a gun now. I've cut down
a tree. You wouldn't recognize me in town—
my hands lost in my pockets, two disabused tools
I've retired from their life of touching you.

Dear Sarah

The sun was gone when you pointed, the trail
ending where our skis disappeared
under fresh snow. Beneath silent fields,
animals dug for the single nut
burning in its white shell. I understood then
that the thin mandolin of your shadow
cutting across the ice all afternoon
wasn't independent of its owner, that your body's
echo didn't mean you wouldn't leave me.

The bear commits to her sleep below the snow, slows
the beat of her great heart, puts hunger
to rest for a season. I always wanted
a body built to outlast such cold. See
how our reticence was a dangerous thing?
So we now must remember each other,
the promise of each long elk's leg,
hooves delicately printing the drifts, skirting
the rack of antlers that lies frozen in the snow.

Gathering

The salt shaker heart wants to make all the lies come true, wants to make
the horses throwing sparks with their shoes on the scree slope

into deer, wants to make the deer into wolves. It would be easier that way.
Or, if not easier, then better—

to find that what the eye sees is not so much what it desires as what it can
create.

The truth—the small doll of it, the excellent human fingernail saved
whole and sanctified—is that I do not love you.

Gather it into the satchel: quince, apple, pear. Then try to tell the tongue
to correct the eye, the hand to speak for the nose.

III

Desire

I can't tell the difference anymore
between what I want and why I want it:
the white, clapboard house in the country
or the husband and children
who wait on its porch; a man with a truck
or our frank heterosexuality. Hunger
hasn't gotten a very good name around here.
And when I do get what I want—
constellations unfurled in one loose rag,
Orion's little, three-hole-punch belt
accompanying each of my first kisses—
it never seems to be enough.
What is it the experts say about desire?
It is not an appetite: it is essentially insatiable.
I want to be a woman held by a man
who stands on the long, metal back of a suspension bridge
lit by a barrel-chested moon. Romance
doesn't begin to describe the kind of tenderness
that can take a brave man—one who has fired a gun,
who knows the frets and grooves
of persistent calluses, who wears a scar that winks
like a pale, forgotten star on his cheek—
and make it impossible for him to touch me.

A Farewell (Composed in Great Advance of the End)

Darling,
give me something to forget you by.

What good are memories
of lip or thigh? Cast in their vat of bluing, the limb-white
sheets still yellow with regret. As time makes waste,
so the tailor plies chalk to mark the cuffs of my too-long pants
and overnight—or even in an afternoon!—the length
comes away, the present suddenly fitting me better
than the past.

Oh, please dismiss the harsh embarrassment
of failing at love's work.

Your absence makes another scrap
of cloth cleaved to memory's quilt. Let it warm us without guilt.
We've a long, cold night to spend our lives apart.

Fourth of July

If I have any romantic notions left,
please let me abandon them here
on the dashboard of your Subaru
beside this container of gas station
potato salad and bottle of sunscreen.
Otherwise, my heart is a sugar packet
waiting to be shaken open by some
other man's hand. Let there be another town
after this one, a town with an improbable Western
name—Wisdom, Last Chance—where we can get
a room and a six-pack, where the fireworks
end early, say nine o'clock, before it's really
gotten dark enough to see them because
everyone has to work in the morning.
I'm not asking for love anymore.
I don't care if I never see a sailboat again.

At Stanfield Reservoir and Wildlife Preserve

Like most places on the map,
we didn't notice it until we were there,
seeing water before it could be seen:

the gathered cottonwoods and willows
telling us everything about the twisted
searchings of buried roots,

thirst, being moored
just at the edge of what you need.
I don't remember parking the car

or letting the dog off his lead—
we were so ready for good fortune.
The night before, paper roses fading

on the motel walls as we slept,
I'd dreamt your hands sifting over me
like dun-colored fish in a lake

of their own choosing. But in daylight
we couldn't find the water, each trunk
carrying the muddied mark of it

right at the height of your shoulder, the place
I lean when I want you to look at me:
bottle caps, shotgun shells, every shade

of broken glass scattered between the downed
trees, a sort of quickening of light
among their limbs.

You fingered the pieces, dust hovering the heat
like mist or a glitter of fine
insects. That dirt road we'd taken

for no reason, the green slick and sheen
of alfalfa fields beneath irrigation pipes,
water pumped from a reservoir going dry—

I wanted to remind you I was there, but not
for always. We heard children, their voices tinkling
like coins fallen down the airless chute

of a slot machine, *Over here! Over here!*
I don't know what they saw, though we heard
their splashing, mistook it for our own.

I Arrive in Paris on the First Day of Montana's Fishing Season

Slick-bellied, the plane, in drizzle and steam.
Understand me when I say this: Time

is the compartment into which I'm putting you.
Before tickets, before tray tables. Here

I'll find the streets glassy and the Dior coats
on last winter's sale rack just as sleek and black

as the pelt of that wolverine we found
on Rock Creek in January. Let's say

time is a fish and she swims in every stream
and you can't catch her, not with the sharpest

barbs of your hooks, not with sink-line
or waders, not with your caddis patterns

or skwala nymphs. She won't take the flies
you've tied with your own hands. I've been

trying to explain this all along. Remember
when we promised to hike every ridgeline

hugging the valley? Here I plan to climb
every stairwell. It may take me years.

On Sunday

Went down to the river.
Heard a plane but didn't see it.
An invisible man in the sky—

I've read about him.
He's supposed to be watching us.
So I took off all my clothes

and got in: green water
seeping up my spine, making me
less than heavy. I told myself

it was his hands untying the knot
like apron strings at my back.
Shuck me, I thought. When it got

cold, I drove into town and stopped
at a bar, the first one
I could find. It wasn't hard

drinking my beer and easing coins
in the jukebox. Sometimes you can't
intellectualize need. A beer,

a song. You put it in the body
and the body makes use of it.
What I needed was a dance,

a lover, a good night's sleep,
not wheel-well circles under
my eyes or sermons about sparrows.

When I got home it was dark,
the hammock swinging on the porch
like a crippled moon. No one

was coming to give me what I
needed, but I lay down and waited
anyway, the air hovering,

as always, just above me.

Memory, Eight Years Old

The neighborhood boys are smiling
when they say they're going to get knives
and come after me. I go into the house
and find my mother at the stove.
I ask her for the sharpest knife she has
but all she'll give me is a plastic picnic spoon.
She laughs, tosses carrots in the pot,
and when I ask her for something more
to protect me from what's coming
she pushes onions, pink cubes of ham
from a heavy plate into the boiling broth.
She doesn't turn her head. So what
strange courage sends me from her house?
Her blue apron swings away as I take the spoon,
examine its opaque curve in the kitchen light,
touch it to my lips where it bends at the neck.
When I step outside, the boys are waiting in the yard.
I can't see what they have flashing in their hands.
I let them chase me into the woods.
Dead leaves fly like sparks under my heels.

You Loved a Woman Once

She told you of childhood summers, mayflies trembling
beside the bridge of her nose, hunting frogs. Skinning them
on a brick, the house smelling like their small, fried legs.

All she wanted was for you to carry her home in a canoe
with paddles, life vests, a flare. You promised
to teach her how to swim when she was in your arms.

Your own body, broken into so many times, became a clear lake
for her to bathe in. Remember pulling the one tiny, suckering
leech from below her neck, the pale collarbone braille it left.

You said the boat was her shoulder in your mouth, even when
you couldn't bear her epaulets of freckles, even when nothing
but a body would do and there was no body but her own.

Below her—lily pads, dragonflies, the worms
dug up last summer and thrown from the dock to see fish
rise in a boil—now all snapped raw in the frozen pond. And speaker,

coded "you"—what about the light straining through her dampened
hair, will you catch it in your jaws? There's the smell of paper
on her skin and you pressing her body like a flower in a book.

Motel

It was a six-hour layover
in the midst of a long-distance
love affair. We'd be in the same
city for exactly a quarter
of a day: one of those motels
just outside the thick spatter
of Newark Airport's lights.
A desk clerk who wouldn't
look us in the eyes and then,
when he did, gave us a brazen
stare. White girl. Black boy.
A room for just an hour.
When I flicked on the light,
our irises shrunk back like
clouds moving toward a storm,
and we saw it for what it was—
the lamp without its shade,
a bedspread like a patch
of flowers freshly trampled.
We couldn't help ourselves,
it was perfect, we wanted
to stay there forever, undressing
under the light of a bare bulb,
pressing each other into
the gritty, worn sheets,
our wrecked form like the junked
cars parked on the turnpike pullouts.
This was the real destination—
the sweat spread on our faces
like some vast Turner landscape—

though we'd try to recreate this scene
in other distant cities, to manufacture again
that same sense of a desperate ending.

Memorial Day

Plant dander spins the air, wind spitting sawdust curls across my windshield like star-shards blown out a comet's ass.

The President's on the radio again, making jokes with his press corps, using the nicknames he's given them.

I'm driving west, cutting down back roads past mud-rutted pig farms and hills studded with tree stumps—the natural, misshapen wreckage of our human work.

All year I've lied to my doctor, perfected the art of nonchalance. Or I've told her the truth, but giggled when she asked questions. Sheepish is an appropriate adjective. She might say cavalier.

I pass a field where black and white heifers glow in the just-dead sun like chess pieces forgotten and abandoned mid-game.

The President's laughing so hard now (he's made a brilliant pun) that he doesn't hear their questions: *But Mr. President, if I could direct your attention back to—*

Last week my gynecologist showed me pictures she took of my uterus: scar tissue wisping up like signal fire smoke and in other spots black holes stretched on my flesh.

I'm like a dog who trashes the house and then cowers when her master comes home: I'm always ready to deny exactly what I'm guilty of.

I pull the car over next to a drainage ditch, turn off the radio. I can hear the wind now, moving its big hands over the roof, fingering the door handles as if their smallness makes them precious.

Intention doesn't really matter once you've been charged with a crime. All the evidence only makes you feel more far away, like you're looking at a picture of a red moon in another galaxy, one with a problem you don't know anything about.

Finally

It's summer. Eighty-five degrees.
We've spent all day on a blanket
in the high grass of an abandoned
cemetery. The backs of my thighs
are sunburned and tomorrow I'll shiver
as the heat pours out of my skin.
Earlier, when I climbed onto you
for the second time, I could see
a row of headstones through the trees.
And when I rocked over you
their round and rain-worn scalps
rose into my line of sight until
I could imagine the bodies beneath them
propped up, watching us make love.
Each one of their wide skulls silently
smiled as if remembering something
sweet and fleeting, and not wanting
to tell me so. I needed to explain to them then
that my body has been a bell
that's waited years to be rung by you.
That the cartilage grinding in my hip sockets
when I move against you makes a dust
finer than the finest semolina flour
and I pay it out from my body willingly.
That finally coming to love you
has been a hard-earned pleasure,
so that every time you enter me
I want to cry out, *Bury me,*
bury me. Put me in the ground.

IV

The Undeniable Desire for Physical Contact Among Boys of a Certain Age

They can't keep their hands off each other, irresistible,
the hard, narrow barbs of their hips, the feet
long, having already outgrown the body
in a fit of physical genius. New muscles are forming
like buds every night in the seams of their flesh
till they wake to a flower that still lacks a certain
metronome for the glory of its bloom. These boys
scoff at the idea of desire, punish those who succumb
to its hum, but the thin beams of their fingers fall
in searchlights on flanks and sweat-filigreed brows,
they brush lips to an ear and out tumbles breath
they know they can't hold. Every nimbus of laughter
encircles an incomplete touch, a hand on a knee, a tongue
in the air, the divining rod wending one from the other.

The Lake Oswego Girls' Soccer Team
at the Hilton Pool

I cannot stop watching their sylph-bodies
leave and return to the water, each nub
of soft flesh, their dimpled hides.
They're playing Marco Polo,
screaming out colors—*purple, turquoise,*
gold—sending bright sparks of water
over our heads. As each takes a turn
standing on the edge of the pool,
I get to watch their bodies at a stage of rupture—
or is it rapture?—the ferocious budding
so young it's not begun yet
to collapse in on itself, each fragment
still holding to the unfinished form. I can't remember
when my body didn't look the way it does now,
fully broken open, split up the middle
and pouring out. They still believe
their bodies are their own,
that they are shaping themselves, choosing the form
they'll take, as if they could know
the curve of the palm that will cup their breasts,
how their bodies will work to receive
another. Even this, they think they will decide.
Why would they doubt their own flesh?
What do they know of betrayal?

If We Do This Thing Together, You and I

At the minor league game where I blush for
the teenage girl who trills our anthem through
her nose and you eat three sausages, or
four, without spilling on your perfect blue
T-shirt, there are no reasons to be too
unhappy, not with children who loudly
beg for cotton candy or umpires who
call out our favorite batter, or lastly
the girl in green-rimmed glasses who sadly
forgets to bring the beer. So why do the
innings seem to take so long? As flatly
played as the whistle from your lips. I see
the mascot wave his arms but I don't cheer.
Like you, I'm trying to forget I'm here.

Ne Me Quitte Pas

I think I've been sad for a long time now—
        crying in my coffee near the Place des Vosges,
        taking pictures of toy sailboats at the Jardin

du Luxembourg as they drift past on their spumes
        of puddle water. Nothing seems to help,
        not eating raspberries from Morocco,

not securing the long, toothlike buttons of my
        winter peacoat, not even knowing how
        during the war, when every kind of citizen put

his neighbor on a train to the chambers, the French
        still kept the trees of Paris trimmed in perfect
        cubes like sugar for espresso. Life doesn't

have to change to get worse. Just keep paying the bills
        and walking the dog. Meet, marry, then
        one of you goes up in smoke. I see

the boot prints in the garden, the twisting pattern
        stamped in the mud, but ignore them for
        the trees that have been cut back as they

should. When the gardener returns, he'll be the same
        boy who however many years ago scattered
        pigeons in the square in front of Notre Dame.

Reading Sappho in a Wine Bar

Today I promised you a poem entitled
"Mowing the Lawn Out of Spite"
in honor of your husband who would
do any job poorly if it might twist

your heart open to him. The wine glasses
are lined up so perfectly. Hard to believe
they might ever be broken, but each one will.
Think of the delicate, the fragile, the weak:

a beetle's wing, a swing's slow arc, your very
smallest child. You watched your husband drag
the lawn mower across the backyard, saw
his lips curse it through the window each time

it stalled. If you listened closely you could
hear his voice, the sound of glass cracking
beneath your feet. Or perhaps he was cursing
you, your joy on this first day of spring.

After Another Argument I've Come to Regret

I've hung a severed deer leg in the tree behind the house
        so that the dogs, sweet demons, don't get into it again

and return to gnawing the hair and gristle and rotten flesh
        from the bone. When you and I fight, and sometimes

we fight all the time—politics, toilet seats, and the truer
        contentions they stand in for—I want to walk to the tree

and see again how dark appetites have forced me to discard
        a limb in the crook of an alder at the base of a hill

so crossed with game trails they appear as stretch marks
        on a giant, hay-colored breast. The proverbs

I remember say *tenderness, mercy*. Make it the leg
        of a child, the perfect black hoof become a pale

sickle of what was such new skin. And the dogs no less
        hungry, no less ready to take their meal.

Hurricane

After the storm, my brother went to New Orleans
to work demolition. He's a skinny 6'2",
so you have to picture him suiting up like an astronaut
in the giant Hazmat gear, long arms and legs
encased in blue plastic as he waded through the wasteland
of street garbage, a red cross stamped on his back.
His crew was assigned to gutting houses in the Lower
Ninth Ward. Each morning they would pull on
face masks and steel shank boots,
climb into the back of a pickup truck and drive east
toward the broken levee and row-houses
hanging onto their foundations
by a few bright threads of insulation. Inside
they tore out the cabinets and appliances, pushed
furniture through windows and onto the sidewalk,
rolled up the carpet where a dog had died,
water's cruel molecule welding its limbs to the rug.
And the water was everywhere, in the light fixtures,
the clogged bathtubs, even an unbroken row of glasses
on the top shelf in the kitchen. He only saw
one resident his whole time there, a man
who told him he was lucky—a white boy—to even
see this neighborhood. But the scariest thing
was the lack of women, only a city of men. And at night
when his crew drove back to their base
through the ravaged, abandoned streets, there were no kids
on the swing sets, the shops standing open but empty, not even the relief
of military personnel positioned on the corner—
they'd taken their machine guns and gone home.
Even so, he said it must be what war is like:

sudden desertion, irreconcilable absence.
One day he opened a closet and discovered
one hundred pairs of women's shoes, silt-soaked
but intact, lined up perfectly, the heels
in back of the flats. He carried them all
out into the street—the spoon still in the sugar bowl, a roll of condoms
tucked in the dresser, the keys he found hanging from a lock.

Proper Etiquette on a Spirit's Return

The phantom sounds have become more frequent:
whistling in the walls, shouting in the barn, the echo
of hammer and saw coming from the woods. No one's
there, I've looked. But still, I hear them. The neighbors
say men are buried on the land, assure me their ghosts
mean no harm. Even my mother suggests believing in
reincarnation, what she calls the recycling of souls.
But what if I believe that we all go down into some
cold, dark death and that a few of us—and I don't mean
the lucky ones—claw our way out of it? What if
they're haunting themselves but we're the ones
who have to give them what they need? Like my friend
who came back from his third tour in Iraq and wanted
to sleep with me. So I let him, I had to. I'm saying
he'd been dead and then there he was alive. How else
do you say thank you? I've thanked men for less: dinner,
a ride home. He came back alive. I had to remind him of that.

After We Say Goodbye

I'm collecting calamities—the eviction notice, snow in June—
anything to distract me from the sad, thin girls who jog
each evening, the odometers of ambulances turning
all over town, the lines between my brows like the kanji

character for rain. I was so happy once wearing a swimsuit.
We get older, walk out of each other's lives like collarless dogs,
become fodder for the past. So lay me to rest like a well-loved
mummy, with buckets of honey and bags of rice. Then use me

to tell your stories, like a character glimpsed from a speeding
car. I'll be the small girl standing tiptoe on a stool
at the firecracker stand. I'll wear that dirty dress over
mosquito-bitten calves until even your tongue rusts to red grain.

Oregon Spring

In the gully where last winter
the tourist died, wild yellow irises
crease the hillside with their brown-veined
palms. The papers said they found him
facedown in the spring-fed creek. I know
the place where its bubbling starts,
water like a still-new scar in the granite.
If beauty doesn't matter, then what does?
I'm glad at least one man didn't die
in an uglier place. His daughters
will visit here one day and remember
his crimson vest, the way it seemed
to glow as he moved away from them
through the snow and the lovely trees—
sugar pine, madrone—they'll still have no names for.

Prayer

Perhaps as a child you had the chicken pox
and your mother, to soothe you in your fever
or to help you fall asleep, came into your room
and read to you from some favorite book,
Charlotte's Web or *Little House on the Prairie*,
a long story that she quietly took you through
until your eyes became magnets for your shuttering
lids and she saw your breathing go slow. And then
she read on, this time silently and to herself,
not because she didn't know the story,
it seemed to her that there had never been a time
when she didn't know this story—the young girl
and her benevolence, the young girl in her sod house—
but because she did not yet want to leave your side
though she knew there was nothing more
she could do for you. And you, not asleep but simply weak,
listened to her turn the pages, still feeling
the lamp warm against one cheek, knowing the shape
of the rocking chair's shadow as it slid across
your chest. So that now, these many years later,
when you are clenched in the damp fist of a hospital bed,
or signing the papers that say you won't love him anymore,
when you are bent at your son's gravesite or haunted
by a war that makes you wake with the gun
cocked in your hand, you would like to believe
that such generosity comes from God, too,
who now, when you have the strength to ask, might begin
the story again, just as your mother would,
from the place where you have both left off.

V

After the Ruins of an Oregon Homestead

Of course there is, for our own short lives, some
mortal terror, which grows now like a man's
abandoned grapevine, his body still ripe
beneath its fragrant leaves. And who's to count
how many have gone under some dream's stiff
wheel and turned the soil or taken root in
ruts carved there? We are, none of us, native
to the earth, not born in the dirt of her
cupped palm, though yes, we go back to it. Oh,
the living with their jars of plums, tomatoes,
bear meat packed in tins, a sack of
semolina flour tipped across the boards—it's
hard to understand how something so quiet
could have been made between two chafing hands.

Waltz of the Midnight Miscarriage

My little empire goes to sleep around me.
The cupcake frosting softens in the streetlamp's
yellow light. The beer cools in the fridge.
Bugs swirl to a delicate halt around the bulbs
of my many lamps—leggy halos—and I wonder,
what does it feel like, the helix of heat
they weave to their burning death?
The clock waltzes toward one and I tick
in my bed, an untethered cable, a live wire
dangling in this kingdom of still
thievery. Even the one who bleeds out
between my legs is silent tonight, her pulse
undone from my own heart's beating. The goblet
drips dry slowly, the cut flowers crumble
ever inward. A small death. Bobby pins
scattered, their numbered litmus,
across the wooden field of the bureau.

The Body or Its Not

I have plans to kill a creature. The best
I can explain it is: I'm afraid. Of what
will be left—a hoof, the jaw, one sun-dried-
soft-as-oats ear. That walking through the woods
next year I'll find these easy relics
and be reminded that winter trees are
not skeletons, that every metaphor
for death deals in blood and bone and our stunned
approximation of their sudden absence.
What's the difference between a body
we love and the trappings that make it?
My soldier who returns home without his
hands, the fingers somewhere else still doing
their slow work of pulling a trigger.

What I Know

Lilies scent the hallway with the death
of beautiful things. A pork chop fries
on its own in the kitchen. Furniture
grows larger in the darkening rooms.
Should I describe the fruit in the bowl?
The hot breath of the lamp beside me?
You know all of this. Below my feet
the moles dig deeper, searching
towards the core. Do they hear the Earth
turning, sense the heat close beneath them?
That's what it was to share a bed, to know
the one still point I moved towards, circling
through the strata of my own grave earth.
The bird you named knows to sing at dusk.
What do I know? Not the rise and fall
of bow against violin. Not the many names
for herbs that join the twilight. Certainly not
that what is dead will live again.

Back from the Cemetery

Our shadows like faithful dogs
who follow us across the snow.
Except that we cannot praise them.
Except that on the coldest morning
we cannot gut them and feed our bodies
with their loyal hearts, warm our hands
in the shallow cavity their lives have left.
It's the same with your red truck
still parked in the driveway when I
get home. What good does it do me
to run the engine? I want you back.
Even if it had everything to do
with saving myself, I loved the way
those dogs came when we called.

My First Lover Returns from Iraq

Despite all these years of not loving you,
you've become the man I build
every poem from, your naked shape
the clay I mold to place at the base of a tree
or in the soft folds of a morning bedroom.
I make your hands into fruit and set them
in bowls, your feet flower from the ends
of frayed pants. In my poems I'm unable
to mend them. Sometimes you walk, usually
you don't speak. I can't seem to give you the words
though all I want is to hear your voice.
What I'm afraid to write is what I dream
at night, when you come to me of your own desire.
And I'm ashamed to want you still, inside me
now as you were then, though you've been
dead these three months, the shrapnel
strung through your lungs like ribbon,
dust filling the reddest caverns of your flesh.
I was the last to be told. And yours
is the only body that visits me now:
your sweat-laden skin, the light it makes
for itself, as if in that darkened room
you had gathered every burning object to you
and you alone shone.

Ikebana for the Dead

The wind outside our apartment
starts like an engine in the leaves,
your voice below it, dropping secrets
in a pale bucket. The chrysanthemums
from the dingy shop in Chinatown
press their blunt white heads together,
and my fingertips rummage their petals
until I'm dirty with scent and they carry my dust.
I prop the green stalks against each other,
the fever of my fingers torturing their leaves,
pruning the long stem of sorrow. The blooms
are palms arranged in your hair, fingers like coral
budding, opening to cradle where you unwind
into curls of burnt umber, unleashed on the sheets.
I won't speak of how each body makes its own dust.
I breathe yours into my lungs every day, each inhalation
sewing me to my gloom with the tight stitches
of final absence. Instead, I speak of the bodies
that have come to do their work in the daylight,
how I now strip off their leaves, arrange their necks
in a delicate latticework. Let me step off this edge,
enter the moment where I choose to speak
a language of grief I still don't understand.
Like every wedding band in every pawnshop,
its worth on the back of a pink receipt
in the bottom of some closet, a shoebox
full of numbers, not the dried blossoms
arranged in a marriage bouquet and not words
somehow still beautiful in the mouth.

Lessons in Psychoanalysis

The first time your son
saw himself in a mirror,
you were holding him
in your arms. It was midwinter,
the apartment on 175th Street,
he couldn't have been more
than four months old. And it was just
as those Lacanian textbooks had described:
he looked from the mirror to you
and back to the mirror, and you told him,
Yes, that's you, that's you.
You allowed him to push away,
to begin the formation of a self
distinct from your hands and mouth, from the eyes
that fed his desires. And for the first time
you actually believed you were that mother
who stood in the mirror.
Because that's what mothers do,
they give things away, milk from the breast,
a necklace laced with bobbles, hours from a life
that can't be brought back. They give away
their children, too, their first born
son, sometimes. None of it
was for nothing. Somewhere
his little wholly formed soul
spins knots in time, travels back
to that mirror, recreates the first glimpse
and begins again. What you can't trace back to,
can't disregard, is yourself. Even with the baby
buried out in Westchester, you still
dance in front of the window at night,

clutching anything willingly helpless,
a loaf of bread, a rolled-up
blanket, whatever looks right
in the wavering glass. Those textbooks
were wrong. There's nothing
about the process of mourning
that feels healthy. Freud
can have his theories.
Something small grows in you now
but it's not made of light, has never seen itself
in a mirror, doesn't know
the ache of eyes against flesh.

Barn Elegy

Before I'm through the door
I can hear them stomping in their stalls,
feet shuffling in church
below the chant of psalms.

There's a brass plaque on each stall door
but I know them by the weight
of their knees, the deep curve of withers,
a gray forelock and its wide spate

of freckles holy in their constellations.
Saints have never looked so real,
the warm flesh, alfalfa sweat slicking
my fingers as I brush the corporeal

coat, the laying on of hands, then bridle.
Virgil canters the arena's soft groove,
his large feet never stumbling, turning
clods of dirt with his elegant hooves.

Later I will take them on my palm. And even
though I hold the reigns, I know I'm not
the master here. The riding hat and crop just
a costume like any other, as simple as the plot

of the fastened seat belt, the small white pill,
the deadbolt slid, or the angling forceps.
I can't possibly save myself.
But I can put a bit to Harley's lips

and he will take it on his tongue,
I can tighten the girth around his ribs
and he will not move away from me,
lean into his shoulder until he lifts the jib

of his leg and lets me take his right front hoof
in my palm, unload his shoes of their heavy oil,
let slip through my fingers
their bitter, worm-dark freight of soil.

Making Love After the Death

It was an artichoke we pulled from the ground
that night. I remember the way you held
the dark beer in your mouth, made the garden
wait for you until you waded in
waist deep. Grasses hugged your long thighs
and you turned among them, a grain of sand
in a moving sea. The baby had been dead a week.
Outside, the moonless sky was alive
with the symphonies of a thousand shuttered
lights. I remember your smooth hands
at the base of the stalks, the care you took
in lifting them from the earth. I wondered
at the gentleness of death at night
when the weight of the moon is absent
and the streetlight does not reach our window.

What Afterlife

Twilight might be called
        a gray scarf pulled over your lover's eyes.
And the bicyclist's body
        cutting swiftly through it

is a beautifully composed semaphore,
        like the shape meaning makes
in a set of signal lights
        at the end of a darkening runway:

two orange sticks crossed, then waving,
        motioning inward.
I should be telling you about fireflies,
        the containment of light, how we work

to bring it closer to us, into our bodies,
        into a glass jar with a screw-on lid
where it can shine and reverberate
        in the ever-thinning air. Instead

I think of my fifth summer,
        the day I lost one shoe
over the side of a sailboat,
        its sinking away from me

into the untreadable dark.
        The soul is composed
of infinite planets sucked into black holes
        and what comes out the other side—

light or its golden shadow—is each our own.
        Like those fishing boats
that ride out to the world's curve each evening,
        their string of bobbing lamps

nothing more than an infirm constellation
        pinned to your child's ceiling.

De-Icing the Plane

God will steal the birds
from our eyes. As if my body
is already a kind of box
for ashes, my mouth a place
for laying black gauze.
Through the thick plastic window
and its rime of sticky snow,
light enters the cabin
in bone-heavy shafts
outweighing the hands in my lap—
the fat already stripped,
the pale wax of my curled palms.
Soon we will fly.

Acknowledgments

Grateful acknowledgment is made to the editors of the following publications in which these works or earlier versions of them previously appeared:

42opus: "Across a Great Wilderness Without You," "Driving Back into the City," "Self-Portrait with Cockroach," "You Loved a Woman Once";

AGNI Online: "After Another Argument I've Come to Regret";

Apple Valley Review: "At Stanfield Reservoir and Wildlife Preserve";

Barrow Street: "Ne Me Quitte Pas";

Born Magazine: "What Afterlife";

Cider Press Review: "What We Call Indian Summer";

The Cortland Review: "On Sunday";

Ellipsis: "Finding Out I'm Pregnant," "Ikebana for the Dead," "The Light Behind Her Head, the Bright Honeycomb of the Sky";

Faultline: "The Undeniable Desire for Physical Contact Among Boys of a Certain Age";

Green Hills Literary Lantern: "Finally";

Guernica: "The Body or Its Not";

Nimrod: "Barn Elegy," "Lessons in Psychoanalysis," "Memorial Day," "My First Lover Returns from Iraq";

Parthenon West Review: "Diagnosis";

Prairie Schooner: "Reading Sappho in a Wine Bar," "Waltz of the Midnight Miscarriage," "What I Know";

Rattle: "Prayer";

Red Rock Review: "Making Love After the Death";

River Styx: "The Lake Oswego Girls' Soccer Team at the Hilton Pool";

The Southeast Review: "What Afterlife";

Southern Hum: "Hurricane";

West Branch: "Remembering Our Last Meal in New York," "Santeria for the City: Blackout, Summer 2003";

Willow Springs: "Fourth of July," "Oregon Spring."

Recordings of a number of these poems are also available at *From the Fishouse: An Audio Archive of Emerging Poets* (www.fishouse.org). "The Light Behind Her Head, the Bright Honeycomb of the Sky" also appears in *From the Fishouse: An Anthology of Poems That Sing, Rhyme, Resound, Syncopate, Alliterate, and Just Plain Sound Great* (Persea, 2009).

I would like to thank the Vermont Studio Center, Oregon Literary Arts, the Squaw Valley Community of Writers, the University of Oregon, and Soapstone for fellowships which enabled me to complete this work.

In addition, I would like to thank PEN Northwest, along with John Daniel, and Bradley and Frank Boyden, for the Margery Davis Boyden Wilderness Writing Residency. This book would not have been possible without the generous time and solitude given me at the Dutch Henry Homestead.

I would also like to express my gratitude to Nathalie Anderson, Michael Copperman, Natalie Diaz, Gibson Fay-LeBlanc, Kevin A. González, Henrietta Goodman, Natalie Graham, Garrett Hongo, Dorianne Laux, David L. K. Murphy, Natalie Peeterse, Eliza Rotterman, Heather Ryan, Thom Ward, and Marion Wrenn, each of whom has been a reader I could not have done without.

Finally, thanks go to my parents and to my brother Jake, my first and last readers, always.

About the Author

Keetje Kuipers is a native of the Northwest. She earned her BA at Swarthmore College and her MFA at the University of Oregon. She has been the recipient of fellowships from the Vermont Studio Center, Squaw Valley Community of Writers, Oregon Literary Arts, and Soapstone, as well as awards from *Atlanta Review* and *Nimrod*. In 2007 she was the Margery Davis Boyden Wilderness Writing Resident, which provided her with seven months of solitude in Oregon's Rogue River Valley where she composed work that has been published in *Prairie Schooner, West Branch, The Southeast Review,* and *Willow Springs,* among others. Keetje teaches writing at the University of Montana and is currently a Wallace Stegner Fellow at Stanford University. She divides her time between San Francisco and Missoula where she lives with her dog, Bishop, and does her best to catch a few fish.

BOA Editions, Ltd.
The A. Poulin, Jr. New Poets of America Series

Colophon

Beautiful in the Mouth, poems by Keetje Kuipers, is set in Centaur, a digitalized version of the font designed for Monotype by Bruce Rogers in 1928. The italic, based on drawings by Frederic Warde, is an interpretation of the work of the sixteenth-century printer and calligrapher Ludovico degli Arrighi, after whom it is named.

The publication of this book is made possible, in part, by the special support of the following individuals:

Anonymous (2)
Aaron & Lara Black
Gwen & Gary Conners
Mark & Karen Conners
Charles & Barbara Coté in memory of Charlie Coté Jr.
Peter & Suzanne Durant
Kip & Debby Hale
Janice N. Harrington & Robert Dale Parker
Bob & Willy Hursh
Robin, Hollon & Casey Hursh in memory of Peter Hursh
X. J. & Dorothy M. Kennedy
Kristina Montvidas Kutkus
Jack & Gail Langerak
Dorianne Laux & Joseph Millar in honor of Deborah Digges
Peter Makuck
Robert & Francie Marx
Boo Poulin
Steven O. Russell & Phyllis Rifkin-Russell
Peggy Savlov in memory of Debra Audet
Vicki & Richard Schwartz
Pat & Mike Wilder
Glenn & Helen William